Table of Contents

As Easy as 1–2–3

1 **Prepare** the assessment task activity.

2 **Administer** the task and record the student's performance.

3 **Reteach** or provide additional practice using the reproducible activity sheet.

Everything You Need

Each assessment task includes:

- **Scripted instructions**
  for administering the assessment task

- **Full-color mats and cards**
  to engage the student in a specific task

- **Class checklist**
  to record each student's performance

- **Reproducible activity sheets**
  for additional skill practice

When to Conduct an Assessment

You may choose to use assessment tasks in any of the following ways:

- Assess students at the beginning of the school year to determine individual student skill levels.

- Administer an assessment after a specific skill has been taught to help confirm mastery or need for further instruction.

- Assess students throughout the year to monitor progress. Use the correlation chart on page 6 to correlate assessments with your lesson plans.

You may also wish to visit www.teaching-standards.com to view how the skills are correlated to your state's standards.

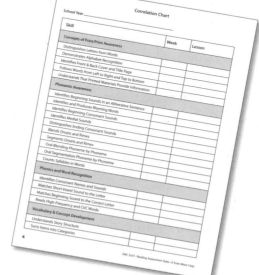

Preparing an Assessment Task Activity

Assemble each assessment task activity and place it in an envelope. Store the envelopes in a file box or crate for easy access.

Materials:
- 9" x 12" (23 x 30.5 cm) large manila envelopes
- scissors
- clear tape
- scripted instructions, manipulatives, class checklist, and activity sheet for the specific assessment task

Steps to Follow:

1. Remove and laminate the *scripted instruction page*. Tape it to the front of the envelope.

2. Remove and laminate the *manipulatives* (sorting mats, task cards, etc.). Store cards in a smaller envelope or plastic bag.

3. Reproduce the *class checklist*. Tape it to the back of the envelope.

4. Make multiple copies of the *activity sheet* and store them in the envelope.

> Make one copy of the *Individual Student Assessment Checklist* (page 5) for each student in your class. You may wish to keep these checklists in a separate binder so they are easily referenced.

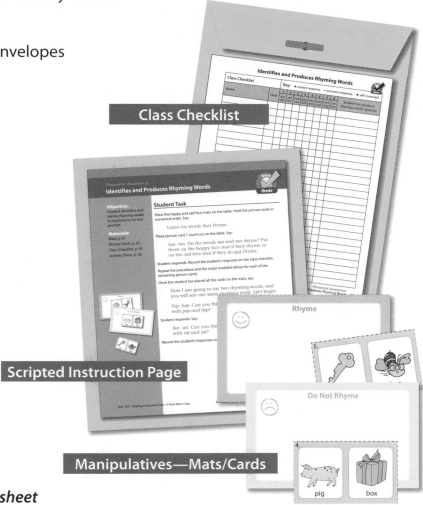

Class Checklist

Scripted Instruction Page

Manipulatives—Mats/Cards

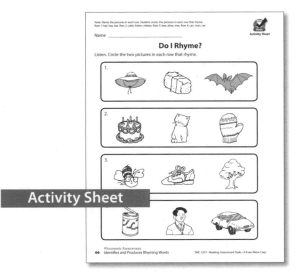

Activity Sheet

How to Conduct an Assessment

- **Be prepared.**

  Preread the scripted instructions. Follow the directions at the top of the script for setting out the cards and mats. Have the class checklist at hand to record the student's responses. Do not ask the student to come to the table until all task materials are in place.

- **Provide a non-threatening atmosphere.**

  The student should complete the task at a quiet, isolated table. Refer to the activity as a "task" or "job," not as a "test."

- **Provide a non-distracting environment.**

  The student should be able to easily focus on the task. Sit next to the student. Communicate in a clear, concise way.

- **Be an unbiased assessor.**

  Do not encourage or discourage or approve or disapprove of the student's responses. Be careful not to use facial expressions that provide feedback.

- **Know when to stop the assessment.**

  Discontinue the assessment activity if it becomes obvious that the student cannot do the task.

- **Be discreet.**

  When recording the student's responses, keep the checklist close to you so it will not distract the student.

What does this mean?

/p/ When a letter is between / /, the letter sound, not the letter name, should be pronounced.

c•at When a bullet appears within a word, emphasize each word part separately.

(ˇ) is used to represent short vowel sounds: căt, gĕt, ĭt, hŏt, pŭp.

(—) is used to represent long vowel sounds: cāke, mē, bīte, hōme, ūse.

Auditory Only Some tasks are auditory only, and are indicated by this icon on the teacher script page. Auditory tasks do not contain mats or task cards.

EMC 3338 • Reading Assessment Tasks • © Evan-Moor Corp.

Individual Student Assessment Checklist

Name _____   School Year _____

Skill	Dates Tested	Date Mastered
Unit 1—Concepts of Print/Print Awareness		
Identifies Letters, Words, and Sentences		
Matches Oral Words to Printed Words		
Demonstrates Print Awareness Skills		
Unit 2—Phonemic Awareness		
Creates and States Rhyming Words		
Discriminates Beginning Sound		
Discriminates Final Sound		
Discriminates Middle Sound		
Discriminates Between Long and Short Vowel Sounds		
Substitutes Initial Sound		
Blends Phonemes into Words		
Orally Segments Words Phoneme by Phoneme		
Counts Syllables in Words		
Unit 3—Phonics		
Identifies Short Vowels		
Identifies Initial and Final Consonant Sounds		
Identifies Long Vowel Sounds		
Identifies the Sounds Made by Long Vowel Digraphs		
Discriminates "R-Controlled" Words		
Reads and Identifies Contractions		
Reads Compound Words		
Reads Inflectional Forms and Root Words		
Reads Common Word Families		
Unit 4—Vocabulary & Concept Development/Reading Comprehension		
Classifies Categories of Words		
Reads High-Frequency Words		
Sequences/Logical Order		
Responds to Who, What, Where, When, and How Questions		
Makes Predictions About What Will Happen Next		

Correlation Chart

School Year _____

Skill	Week	Lesson
Unit 1—Concepts of Print/Print Awareness		
Identifies Letters, Words, and Sentences		
Matches Oral Words to Printed Words		
Demonstrates Print Awareness Skills		
Unit 2—Phonemic Awareness		
Creates and States Rhyming Words		
Discriminates Beginning Sound		
Discriminates Final Sound		
Discriminates Middle Sound		
Discriminates Between Long and Short Vowel Sounds		
Substitutes Initial Sound		
Blends Phonemes into Words		
Orally Segments Words Phoneme by Phoneme		
Counts Syllables in Words		
Unit 3—Phonics		
Identifies Short Vowels		
Identifies Initial and Final Consonant Sounds		
Identifies Long Vowel Sounds		
Identifies the Sounds Made by Long Vowel Digraphs		
Discriminates "R-Controlled" Words		
Reads and Identifies Contractions		
Reads Compound Words		
Reads Inflectional Forms and Root Words		
Reads Common Word Families		
Unit 4—Vocabulary & Concept Development/Reading Comprehension		
Classifies Categories of Words		
Reads High-Frequency Words		
Sequences/Logical Order		
Responds to Who, What, Where, When, and How Questions		
Makes Predictions About What Will Happen Next		

 EMC 3338 • Reading Assessment Tasks • © Evan-Moor Corp.

Unit 1
Concepts of Print/Print Awareness

Concepts of Print/Print Awareness

EMC 3338 • Reading Assessment Tasks • © Evan-Moor Corp.

Identifies Letters, Words, and Sentences

Objective:

Student discriminates between a letter, a word, and a sentence.

Materials:

Mat, p. 11

Class Checklist, p. 13

Activity Sheet, p. 14

Student Task

Place the mat on the table. Say:

> Look at the mat. I'm going to ask you to find some things. Let's begin.

> Point to a box that shows only a letter.

Student responds. Record the student's response on the class checklist. Say:

> Point to a box that shows only a word.

Student responds. Record the student's response on the class checklist. Say:

> Point to a box that shows a sentence.

Student responds. Record the student's response on the class checklist.

Identifies Letters, Words, and Sentences

Identifies Letters, Words, and Sentences

b

go

Run, Sam, run!

red

R

s

I see a dog.

Identifies Letters, Words, and Sentences

Concepts of Print/Print Awareness

EMC 3338 • © Evan-Moor Corp.

Identifies Letters, Words, and Sentences

Class Checklist					
Key:	**+** correct response		**−** incorrect response	**●** self-corrected	

Name	Date	Letter	Word	Sentence	Notes

Name _____

Who Is It?

Color the shapes with a **letter** yellow.
Color the shapes with a **word** blue.
Read the sentence.

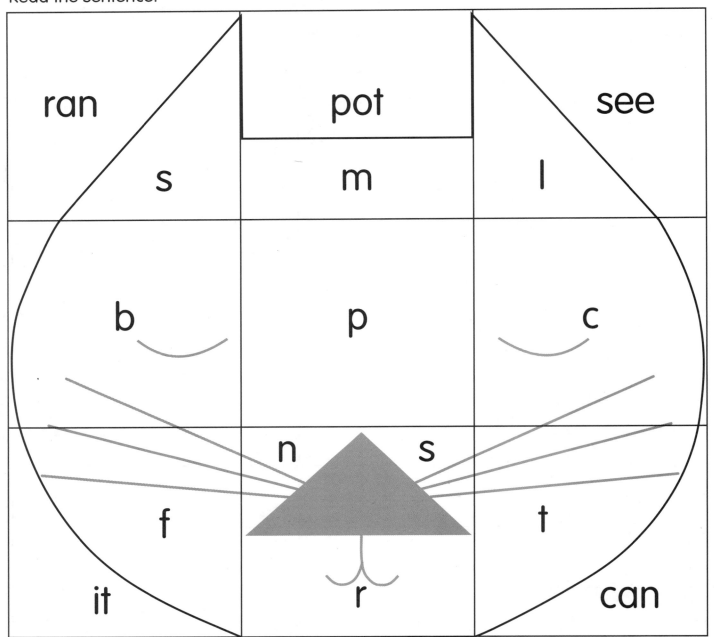

I am a cat.

Matches Oral Words to Printed Words

Objective:
Student displays one-to-one matching from voice to print.

Materials:
Cards, p. 17
Class Checklist, p. 19
Activity Sheet, p. 20

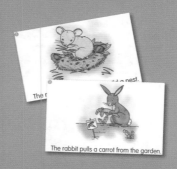

The rabbit pulls a carrot from the garden.

Student Task

Place card 1 on the table. Say:

> I am going to read this sentence to you.
> You point to each word as I read. Let's begin.

Read card 1 aloud.

Record the student's response on the class checklist.

You may wish to repeat the procedure with card 2 or use card 2 for retesting purposes.

1

The mouse uses straw to build a nest.

2

The rabbit pulls a carrot from the garden.

Concepts of Print/Print Awareness
Matches Oral Words to Printed Words

Matches Oral Words to Printed Words

Concepts of Print/Print Awareness

EMC 3338 • © Evan-Moor Corp.

Matches Oral Words to Printed Words

Concepts of Print/Print Awareness

EMC 3338 • © Evan-Moor Corp.

Matches Oral Words to Printed Words

Class Checklist		Key: + correct response — incorrect response ● self-corrected	
Name	Date	Matched Voice to Print	Notes

Concepts of Print/Print Awareness
Matches Oral Words to Printed Words

Note: Read the story to the student. Ask the student to point to each word as you read.

Name _____

Ned

Point to each word as I read. Then color the picture.

See Ned.
See the flower.
Ned waters the flower.

EMC 3338 • Reading Assessment Tasks • © Evan-Moor Corp.

Demonstrates Print Awareness Skills

Objective:

Student identifies author and title. Student performs directionality and return sweep. Student identifies the meaning of basic punctuation marks.

Materials:

Book: *Up and Down*, pp. 23–26

Class Checklist, p. 27

Activity Sheet, p. 28

Auditory Only

Student Task

Place the book on the table. Say:

> I am going to ask to you to show me different parts of this book. Let's begin.

> Point to the title.

Student responds. Record the student's response on the class checklist. Say:

> Point to the author's name.

Student responds. Record the student's response on the class checklist. Say:

> Point to where I start reading the story.

Student responds. Say:

> Now move your finger over all of the words I will read.

Student responds. (You are looking for left-to-right directionality and a return sweep to the beginning of the next sentence.) Record the student's response on the class checklist. If the student did not perform the return sweep, place your finger on the last word of a sentence and say:

> Where do I read next?

Student responds. Record the student's response on the class checklist. Point to a period at the end of a sentence. Say:

> What is this for?

Student responds. Sample responses: *It is a period*. Or, *It ends the sentence*. Record the student's response on the class checklist.

Point to the question mark on page 1. Say:

> What is this for?

Student responds. Sample responses: *It is a question mark*. Or, *You write it when you ask a question*. Record the student's response.

Note: Laminate pages 23 and 25. Cut them out and fold. Place page 25 inside the folded page 23.

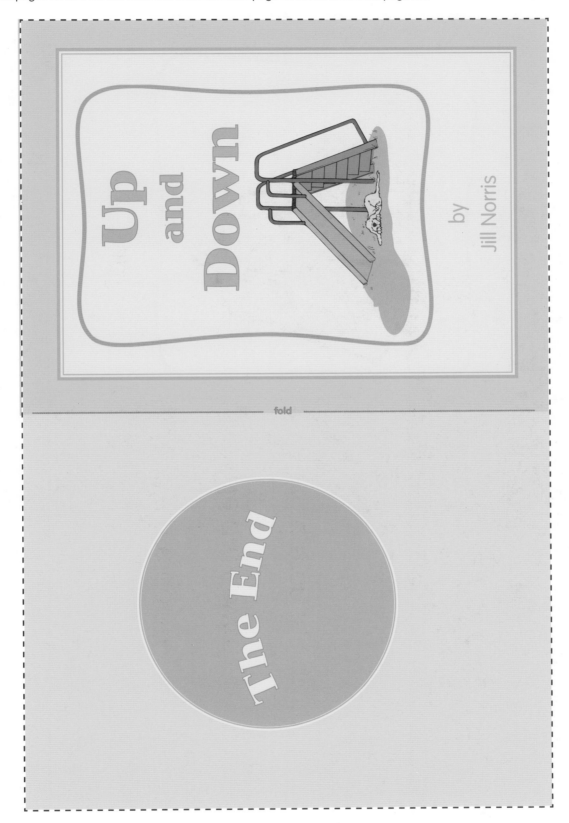

Concepts of Print/Print Awareness
Demonstrates Print Awareness Skills

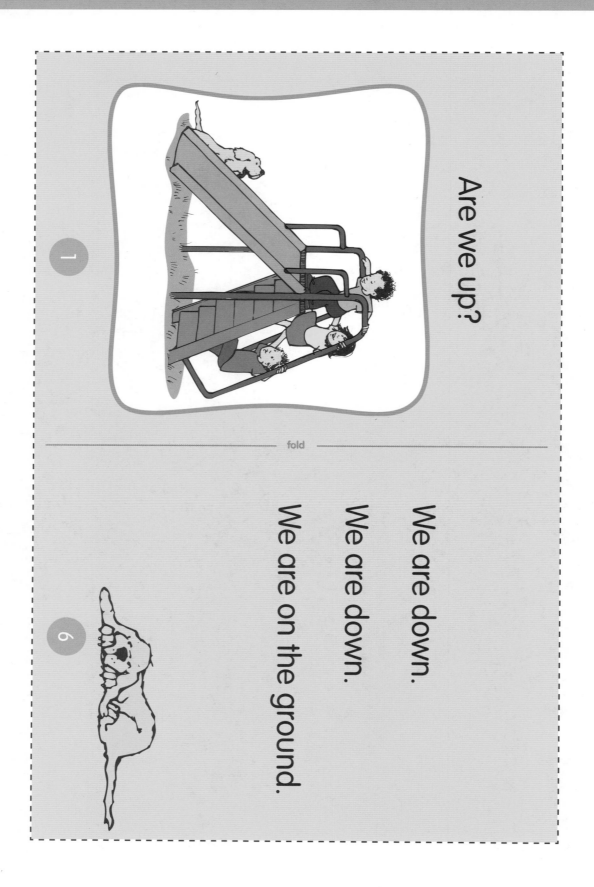

1

Are we up?

fold

6

We are down.

We are down.

We are on the ground.

We are up.

We are up

on the slide.

2

---

fold

Are we down?

5

Concepts of Print/Print Awareness
Demonstrates Print Awareness Skills

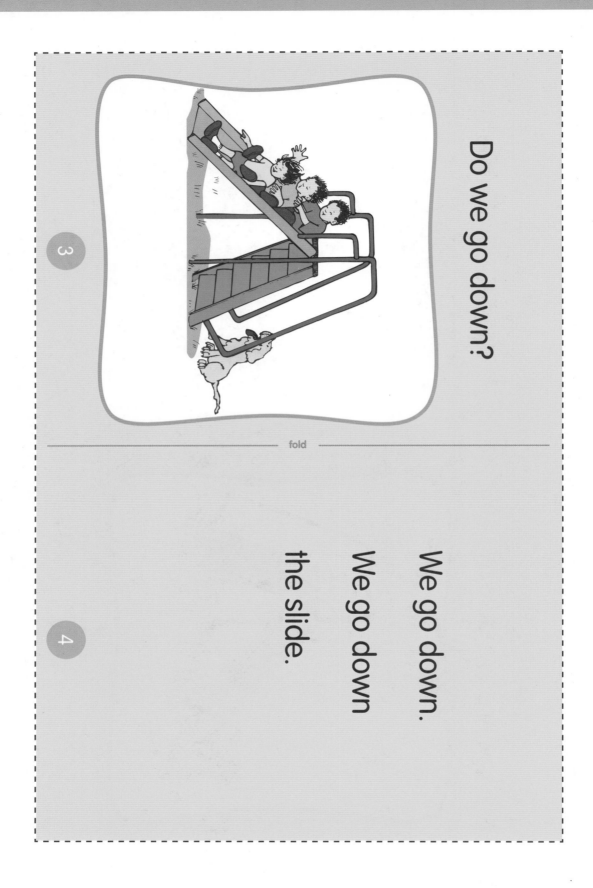

3

Do we go down?

fold

4

We go down.

We go down

the slide.

Concepts of Print/Print Awareness
Demonstrates Print Awareness Skills

EMC 3338 • Reading Assessment Tasks • © Evan-Moor Corp.

Demonstrates Print Awareness Skills

Class Checklist		Key:	+ correct response	— incorrect response		• self-corrected	

Name	Date	Title	Author	Direction-ality	Return Sweep	Period	Question Mark	Notes

Note: Read the book to the student. The student points to each word as you read.

Name _____

My Little Book

Cut out and fold the little book.
Point to each word as I read.

Hen has eggs.

My hen is red.

2

1

fold 2

fold 1   fold 1

3

Hen

Hen has chicks.

Unit 2
Phonemic Awareness

Creates and States Rhyming Words

Objective:
Student orally states rhyming words.

Materials:
Class Checklist, p. 33

Activity Sheet, p. 34

Auditory
Only

Student Task

Say:

> I'm going to say two rhyming words, and then you will add another word. Let's begin.
>
> *sat, hat, _____*

Student responds. Record the student's response on the class checklist. Say:

> Tell me a word that rhymes with
> *wig, pig, _____.*

Student responds. Record the student's response on the class checklist. Say:

> Tell me a word that rhymes with
> *hop, top, _____.*

Student responds. Record the student's response on the class checklist. Say:

> Tell me a word that rhymes with
> *tree, knee, _____.*

Student responds. Record the student's response on the class checklist. Say:

> Tell me a word that rhymes with
> *fun, bun, _____.*

Student responds. Record the student's response on the class checklist. Say:

> Tell me a word that rhymes with
> *goat, coat, _____.*

Creates and States Rhyming Words

Class Checklist		Key: **+** correct response **–** incorrect response **●** self-corrected							
Name	Date	sat hat	wig pig	hop top	tree knee	fun bun	goat coat	Notes/Other Rhyming Words

EMC 3338 • Reading Assessment Tasks • © Evan-Moor Corp.

Phonemic Awareness
Creates and States Rhyming Words
33

Name _____

Rhyming Pairs

Say the names of the pictures.

Color 🙂 if the pictures rhyme.

Color 🙁 if the pictures do <u>not</u> rhyme.

Discriminates Beginning Sound

Objective:

Student orally identifies the initial sound of a given set of words.

Materials:

Class Checklist, p. 37

Activity Sheet, p. 38

Auditory Only

Model the Task

Say:

> I am going to say a group of words that have the same beginning sound.
>
> *fog, fan, fun*
>
> I hear /f/ at the beginning of each word.

Student Task

> Now it's your turn. I will say a group of words and you will tell me what beginning sound you hear. Let's begin.
>
> *map, men, moon*
> What beginning sound do you hear?

Student responds. Record the student's response on the class checklist. Say:

> *sit, sun, surf*
> What beginning sound do you hear?

Student responds. Record the student's response on the class checklist. Say:

> *ten, top, time*
> What beginning sound do you hear?

Student responds. Record the student's response on the class checklist. Say:

> *pig, pan, pick*
> What beginning sound do you hear?

Student responds. Record the student's response on the class checklist.

Discriminates Beginning Sound

Class Checklist		Key:	+ correct response	− incorrect response	• self-corrected

Name	Date	/m/	/s/	/t/	/p/	Notes

Name _____

Beginning Sound

Name each picture.
Circle the letter you hear at the beginning.

1. b s (m)	2. b s m	3. s m t
4. p b s	5. b s m	6. b s m
7. b s m	8. b s m	9. t b m

Objective:
Student orally identifies the final sound of a given set of words.

Materials:
Class Checklist, p. 41
Activity Sheet, p. 42

Auditory Only

Model the Task

Say:

> I am going to say a group of words that have the same ending sound.
>
> *pen, run, man*
>
> I hear /n/ at the end.

Student Task

> Now it's your turn. I will say a group of words and you will tell me what ending sound you hear. Let's begin.
>
> *hop, cup, step*
> What ending sound do you hear?

Student responds. Record the student's response on the class checklist. Say:

> *bug, pig, flag*
> What ending sound do you hear?

Student responds. Record the student's response on the class checklist. Say:

> *red, kid, sled*
> What ending sound do you hear?

Student responds. Record the student's response on the class checklist. Say:

> *sell, bell, fall*
> What ending sound do you hear?

Student responds. Record the student's response on the class checklist.

Discriminates Final Sound

Class Checklist		Key: **+** correct response **−** incorrect response ● self-corrected				

Name	Date	/p/	/g/	/d/	/l/	Notes

Note: Student discriminates the ending sound.
1. dog, 2. foot, 3. cat, 4. leaf, 5. pig, 6. sled, 7. bell, 8. duck, 9. flag

Name _____

Ending Sound

Name each picture.
Circle the letter you hear at the end.

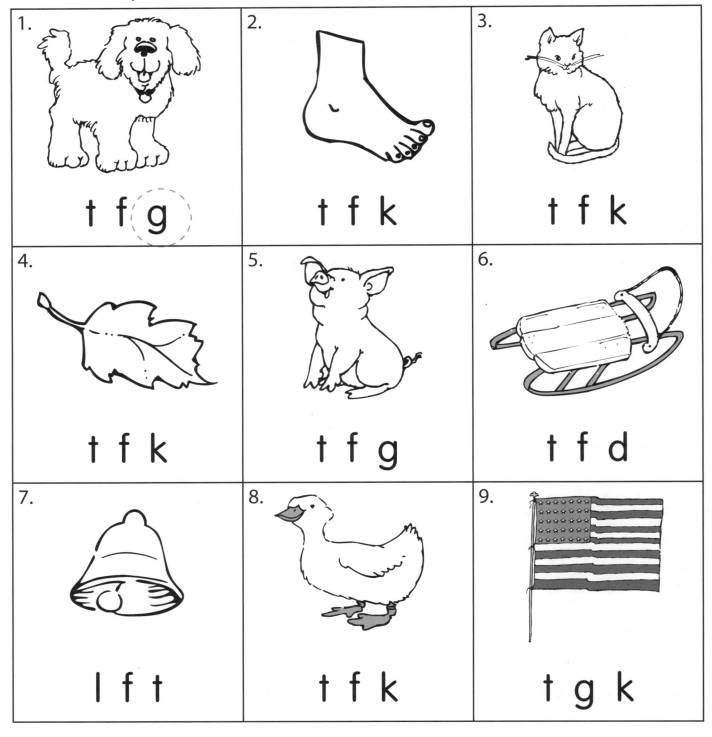

1.	2.	3.
t f (g)	t f k	t f k
4.	5.	6.
t f k	t f g	t f d
7.	8.	9.
l f t	t f k	t g k

Objective:
Student orally identifies the medial sound in a given set of words.

Materials:
Class Checklist, p. 45

Activity Sheet, p. 46

Auditory Only

Model the Task

Say:

> I am going to say a group of words that have the same middle sound.
>
> *set, bed, pet*
>
> I hear /e/ in the middle.

Student Task

> Now it's your turn. I will say a group of words and you will tell me what sound you hear in the middle. Let's begin.
>
> *cat, sap, tab*
> What sound do you hear in the middle?

Student responds. Record the student's response on the class checklist. Say:

> *pot, stop, rod*
> What sound do you hear in the middle?

Student responds. Record the student's response on the class checklist. Say:

> *sit, dig, gift*
> What sound do you hear in the middle?

Student responds. Record the student's response on the class checklist. Say:

> *tub, cup, pup*
> What sound do you hear in the middle?

Student responds. Record the student's response on the class checklist.

Discriminates Middle Sound

Class Checklist		Key: + correct response − incorrect response ● self-corrected				
Name	Date	/ă/	/ŏ/	/ĭ/	/ŭ/	Notes

Note: Student discriminates the middle sound.
1. pin, 2. web, 3. hat, 4. fox, 5. duck, 6. pig, 7. cup, 8. dog, 9. bed, 10. clock, 11. bat, 12. fish

Name _____

In the Middle

Name each picture.
Circle the letter you hear in the middle.

1. i e a	2. i a e	3. e a u
4. u o a	5. o a u	6. e i o
7. e a u	8. e o u	9. e a o
10. u o a	11. a u i	12. a e i

Phonemic Awareness
Discriminates Middle Sound

46

Discriminates Between Long and Short Vowel Sounds

Objective:

Student discriminates between long and short vowel sounds.

Materials:

Mat, p. 49

Picture Cards, p. 51

Class Checklist, p. 53

Activity Sheet, p. 54

Student Task

Place the mat on the table. Hold the picture cards in order (1–4). Say:

> I will say some words, and you will listen closely to the middle sound in each word. Let's begin.

Point to row 1 on the mat. Point to *cat* and *cape* as you refer to them. Place card 1 (cane) on the table. Say:

> *Cane.* Does *cane* have the same middle sound as *cat* or *cape*?

Student responds. Say:

> Put it next to the picture with the same middle sound.

Record the student's response on the class checklist. Point to row 2 on the mat. Place card 2 (red) on the table. Say:

> *Red.* Does *red* have the same middle sound as *hen* or *seed*?

Student responds. Say:

> Put it next to the picture with the same middle sound.

Record the student's response on the class checklist. Point to row 3 on the mat. Place card 3 (fish) on the table. Say:

> *Fish.* Does *fish* have the same middle sound as *pig* or *bike*?

Student responds. Say:

> Put it next to the picture with the same middle sound.

Record the student's response on the class checklist. Repeat the procedure and the script modeled above for row 4 and the remaining picture card.

Long and Short Vowel Sounds

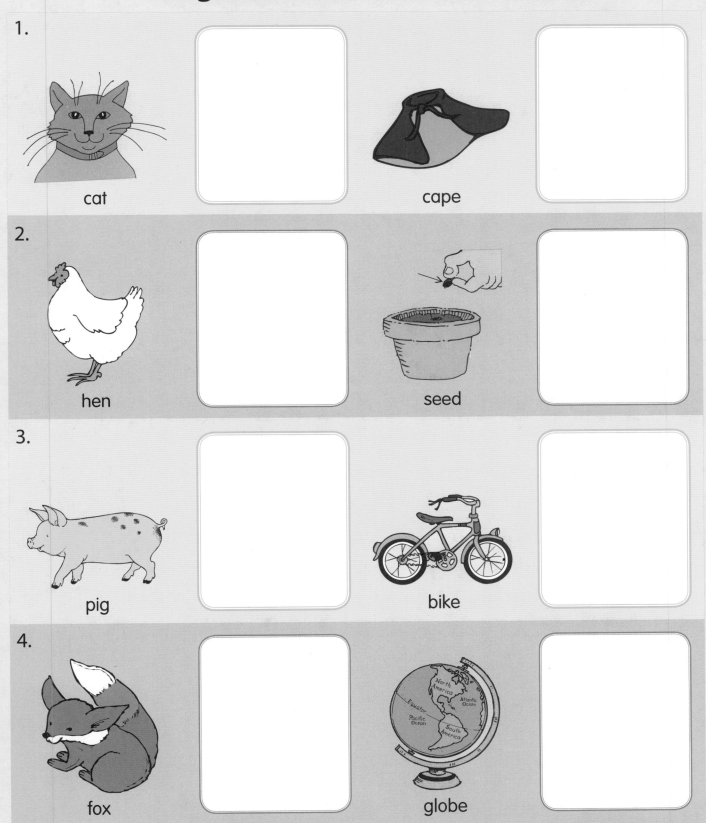

1. cat   cape

2. hen   seed

3. pig   bike

4. fox   globe

Phonemic Awareness
Discriminates Between Long and Short Vowel Sounds

**Discriminates Between
Long and Short Vowel Sounds**
Phonemic Awareness

EMC 3338 • © Evan-Moor Corp.

1. cane
2. red
3. fish
4. boat

Phonemic Awareness
Discriminates Between Long and Short Vowel Sounds

**Discriminates
Between Long
and Short
Vowel Sounds**
Phonemic
Awareness

EMC 3338 • © Evan-Moor Corp.

**Discriminates
Between Long
and Short
Vowel Sounds**
Phonemic
Awareness

EMC 3338 • © Evan-Moor Corp.

**Discriminates
Between Long
and Short
Vowel Sounds**
Phonemic
Awareness

EMC 3338 • © Evan-Moor Corp.

**Discriminates
Between Long
and Short
Vowel Sounds**
Phonemic
Awareness

EMC 3338 • © Evan-Moor Corp.

Discriminates Between Long and Short Vowel Sounds

Class Checklist						Key: **+** correct response **−** incorrect response **●** self-corrected
Name	Date	cane: cape	red: hen	fish: pig	boat: globe	Notes

Note: Student identifies medial sounds.
Row 1: bike, pig, hive. **Row 2:** rose, boat, pot. **Row 3:** bed, bee, red. **Row 4:** bat, hat, rain.

Name _____

Which Sound?

Name each picture.
Circle the picture that has the same middle sound as the first picture.

1. bike

2. rose

3. bed

4. bat

Red

Phonemic Awareness
54 Discriminates Between Long and Short Vowel Sounds

EMC 3338 • Reading Assessment Tasks • © Evan-Moor Corp.

Quick Checks

Activity She

Substitutes Initial Sound

Objective:
Student orally substitutes the initial sound of a given word.

Materials:
Class Checklist, p. 57

Activity Sheet, p. 58

Auditory Only

Model the Task

Say:

> Today we are going to replace the first sound in a word with a different sound. Let's begin.
>
> I will replace the first sound in *cat* with /h/. *Hat.*
>
> I will replace the first sound in *car* with /f/. *Far.*

Student Task

> Now it's your turn.
> Replace the first sound in *mat* with /s/.

Student responds. Record the student's response on the class checklist. Say:

> Replace the first sound in *pig* with /d/.

Student responds. Record the student's response on the class checklist. Say:

> Replace the first sound in *sun* with /r/.

Student responds. Record the student's response on the class checklist. Say:

> Replace the first sound in *top* with /h/.

Student responds. Record the student's response on the class checklist.

Phonemic Awareness
Substitutes Initial Sound

Substitutes Initial Sound

Class Checklist							
Key: + correct response − incorrect response ● self-corrected							
Name	Date	mat to sat	pig to dig	sun to run	top to hop	Notes	

EMC 3338 • Reading Assessment Tasks • © Evan-Moor Corp.

Phonemic Awareness
Substitutes Initial Sound

57

Note: Student matches pictures that sound the same, but have a different beginning sound.
1. hat, 2. bell, 3. van, 4. jam, 5. dog

Name _____

Change It

Name each picture. Draw a line to match pictures that sound the same, but have a different beginning sound.

1.

2.

3.

4.

5.

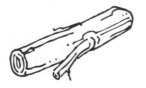

Objective:
Student blends sounds together to form words.

Materials:
Class Checklist, p. 61

Activity Sheet, p. 62

Auditory Only

Model the Task

Say:

I am going to say three word parts. Then I will say the word as a whole.

/c/ /u/ /t/   The word is *cut*.

Student Task

Now it's your turn. I will say three word parts and you will say the word. Let's begin.

/b/ /e/ /d/   What's the word?

Student responds. Record the student's response on the class checklist. Say:

/h/ /a/ /t/   What's the word?

Student responds. Record the student's response on the class checklist. Say:

/m/ /a/ /p/   What's the word?

Student responds. Record the student's response on the class checklist. Say:

/w/ /i/ /g/   What's the word?

Student responds. Record the student's response on the class checklist. Say:

/p/ /o/ /t/   What's the word?

Student responds. Record the student's response on the class checklist.

Blends Phonemes into Words

Class Checklist		Key: + correct response − incorrect response ● self-corrected					
Name	Date	bed	hat	map	wig	pot	Notes

Note: Read the phonemes for each row. Student blends the sounds and circles the correct picture.

Row 1: /c//ā//k/
Row 2: /b//ī//k/
Row 3: /s//p//ōō//n/
Row 4: /t//ō/

Name _____

Listen to the Sounds

Listen to these word parts.
Circle the correct picture.

Phonemic Awareness
Blends Phonemes into Words

EMC 3338 • Reading Assessment Tasks • © Evan-Moor Corp.

Orally Segments Words Phoneme by Phoneme

Objective:
Student listens to a word and then identifies which sounds make up the word and how many sounds he or she hears.

Materials:
Mat, p. 65

Class Checklist, p. 67

Activity Sheet, p. 68

Model the Task

Place the mat on the table. Say:

> I will say a word. Then I will say it sound by sound. I will tell you how many sounds I hear.

Point to picture 1 (rain). Say:

> *Rain.* /r/ /ā/ /n/
> I hear three sounds in the word *rain.*

Student Task

> Now it's your turn.

Point to picture 2 (bike). Say:

> *Bike.* Say *bike* sound by sound.

Student responds. Say:

> How many sounds do you hear?

Record the student's response on the class checklist.

Point to picture 3 (egg). Say:

> *Egg.* Say *egg* sound by sound.

Student responds. Say:

> How many sounds do you hear?

Record the student's response on the class checklist.

Repeat the procedure and the script modeled above for each of the remaining pictures (tie, tub, boat).

Count the Sounds

bike

Orally Segments Words Phoneme by Phoneme

Phonemic Awareness

EMC 3338 • © Evan-Moor Corp.

rain

Orally Segments Words Phoneme by Phoneme

Phonemic Awareness

EMC 3338 • © Evan-Moor Corp.

tie

Orally Segments Words Phoneme by Phoneme

Phonemic Awareness

EMC 3338 • © Evan-Moor Corp.

egg

Orally Segments Words Phoneme by Phoneme

Phonemic Awareness

EMC 3338 • © Evan-Moor Corp.

boat

Orally Segments Words Phoneme by Phoneme

Phonemic Awareness

EMC 3338 • © Evan-Moor Corp.

tub

Orally Segments Words Phoneme by Phoneme

Phonemic Awareness

EMC 3338 • © Evan-Moor Corp.

Orally Segments Words Phoneme by Phoneme

Class Checklist		Key: **+** correct response **−** incorrect response **●** self-corrected					
Name	Date	bike (3)	egg (2)	tie (2)	tub (3)	boat (3)	Notes

Activity She

Name _____

Count the Sounds

Listen to each picture name.
Fill in the circles to show how many sounds you hear.

1.	2.	3.
○ ○ ○ ○	○ ○ ○ ○	○ ○ ○ ○

4.	5.	6.
○ ○ ○ ○	○ ○ ○ ○	○ ○ ○ ○

7.	8.	9.
○ ○ ○ ○	○ ○ ○ ○	○ ○ ○ ○

Model the Task

Place the mat on the table. Say:

> I am going to point to a picture and say a word. I will clap the number of syllables I hear in the word.

Point to picture 1 (table). Say:

> *table*

Clap as you say the word parts. Say:

> Ta•ble. I hear two syllables in the word *table*.

Student Task

> Now it's your turn. I will say a word and you will clap the syllables you hear. Let's begin.

Point to picture 2 (butterfly). Say:

> *Butterfly.* Clap the number of syllables you hear.

Student responds. Record the student's response on the class checklist. Point to picture 3 (apple). Say:

> *Apple.* Clap the number of syllables you hear.

Student responds. Record the student's response on the class checklist. Point to picture 4 (ant). Say:

> *Ant.* Clap the number of syllables you hear.

Student responds. Record the student's response on the class checklist. Point to picture 5 (elephant). Say:

> *Elephant.* Clap the number of syllables you hear.

Student responds. Record the student's response on the class checklist. Point to picture 6 (hat). Say:

> *Hat.* Clap the number of syllables you hear.

Record the student's response on the class checklist.

Objective:
Student claps the syllables in orally stated words.

Materials:
Mat, p. 71
Class Checklist, p. 73
Activity Sheet, p. 74

Counts Syllables

1.

2.

3.

4.

5.

6.

butterfly

Counts Syllables in Words

Phonemic Awareness

EMC 3338 • © Evan-Moor Corp.

table

Counts Syllables in Words

Phonemic Awareness

EMC 3338 • © Evan-Moor Corp.

ant

Counts Syllables in Words

Phonemic Awareness

EMC 3338 • © Evan-Moor Corp.

apple

Counts Syllables in Words

Phonemic Awareness

EMC 3338 • © Evan-Moor Corp.

hat

Counts Syllables in Words

Phonemic Awareness

EMC 3338 • © Evan-Moor Corp.

elephant

Counts Syllables in Words

Phonemic Awareness

EMC 3338 • © Evan-Moor Corp.

Counts Syllables in Words

Class Checklist		Key: + correct response − incorrect response ● self-corrected					
Name	Date	butterfly (3)	apple (2)	ant (1)	elephant (3)	hat (1)	Notes

Name _____

Listen for the Claps

Listen to each picture name.
Clap the syllables.
Circle the number.

1. 1 2 3	2. 1 2 3	3. 1 2 3
4. 1 2 3	5. 1 2 3	6. 1 2 3
7. 1 2 3	8. 1 2 3	9. 1 2 3

Phonemic Awareness
Counts Syllables in Words

EMC 3338 • Reading Assessment Tasks • © Evan-Moor Corp.

Quick Checks

Unit 3
Phonics

EMC 3338 • Reading Assessment Tasks • © Evan-Moor Corp.

Identifies Short Vowels

Student Task

Place the mat on the table. Lay the vowel cards on the table faceup in rows. Point to box 1 on the mat. Say:

> Today you will show me which vowel sounds you hear.
>
> Look at the mat. Each box shows a word that is missing a vowel sound. I will say a word, and you will listen and tell me which vowel sound you hear. Let's begin.

Point to picture 1 (cat) on the mat. Say:

> *Cat.* Which vowel sound do you hear in *cat*?

Student responds orally. Say:

> Place the vowel sound you hear in the square.

Student responds by choosing a vowel and placing it on the mat. Point to picture 2 (pig) on the mat. Say:

> *Pig.* Which vowel sound do you hear in *pig*?

Student responds orally. Say:

> Place the vowel sound you hear in the square.

Student responds. Point to picture 3 (bus) on the mat. Say:

> *Bus.* Which vowel sound do you hear in *bus*?

Student responds orally. Say:

> Place the vowel sound you hear in the square.

Student responds. Repeat the procedure and the script modeled above for the three remaining boxes on the mat. Use the mat as a reference to record the student's responses.

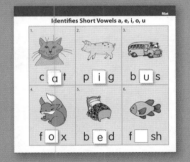

Identifies Short Vowels a, e, i, o, u

Phonics
Identifies Short Vowels

Identifies Short Vowels
Phonics
EMC 3338 • © Evan-Moor Corp.

**Identifies
Short Vowels**
Phonics
EMC 3338
© Evan-Moor Corp.

**Identifies
Short Vowels**
Phonics
EMC 3338
© Evan-Moor Corp.

**Identifies
Short Vowels**
Phonics
EMC 3338
© Evan-Moor Corp.

**Identifies
Short Vowels**
Phonics
EMC 3338
© Evan-Moor Corp.

**Identifies
Short Vowels**
Phonics
EMC 3338
© Evan-Moor Corp.

**Identifies
Short Vowels**
Phonics
EMC 3338
© Evan-Moor Corp.

**Identifies
Short Vowels**
Phonics
EMC 3338
© Evan-Moor Corp.

**Identifies
Short Vowels**
Phonics
EMC 3338
© Evan-Moor Corp.

**Identifies
Short Vowels**
Phonics
EMC 3338
© Evan-Moor Corp.

**Identifies
Short Vowels**
Phonics
EMC 3338
© Evan-Moor Corp.

**Identifies
Short Vowels**
Phonics
EMC 3338
© Evan-Moor Corp.

**Identifies
Short Vowels**
Phonics
EMC 3338
© Evan-Moor Corp.

**Identifies
Short Vowels**
Phonics
EMC 3338
© Evan-Moor Corp.

**Identifies
Short Vowels**
Phonics
EMC 3338
© Evan-Moor Corp.

Identifies Short Vowels

Class Checklist		Key: **+** correct response **−** incorrect response ● self-corrected						
Name	Date	cat a	pig i	bus u	fox o	bed e	fish i	Notes

EMC 3338 • Reading Assessment Tasks • © Evan-Moor Corp.

Phonics
Identifies Short Vowels   **81**

Name _____

Short Vowels
a, e, i, o, u

Name each picture.
Write the short vowel sound you hear.

1. m__p	2. h__n	3. p__g
4. l__g	5. b__s	6. j__t
7. l__p	8. t__p	9. c__p

Identifies Initial and Final Consonant Sounds

Objective:

Student identifies initial and final consonant sounds.

Materials:

Beginning/Ending Cards, pp. 85 and 87

Letter Cards, p. 87

Class Checklist, p. 89

Activity Sheet, p. 90

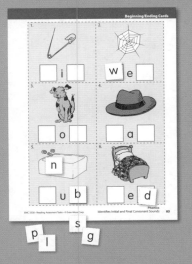

Model the Task

Place card 1 (pin) on the table. Place the letter cards on the table faceup in rows. Say:

> Today you will show me the first and last sounds you hear in a word. I will show you what to do.

> This picture shows a pin. Listen to the word *pin*.

Place the letter *p* in the first box on card 1. Say:

> /p/ is the first sound I hear in *pin*.

Place the letter *n* in the last box on card 1. Say:

> /n/ is the last sound I hear in *pin*.

Student Task

Clear card 1. Return the letter cards to their rows. Place card 2 on the table. Say:

> Now it's your turn. Listen to the word *web*.

> Choose the letter that stands for the first sound you hear. Place it in the first box.

Student responds. Say:

> Choose the letter that stands for the last sound you hear. Place it in the last box.

Student responds. Record the student's responses on the class checklist.

Clear card 2. Return the letter cards to their rows. Place card 3 on the table. Repeat the procedure and the script modeled above for each of the remaining cards.

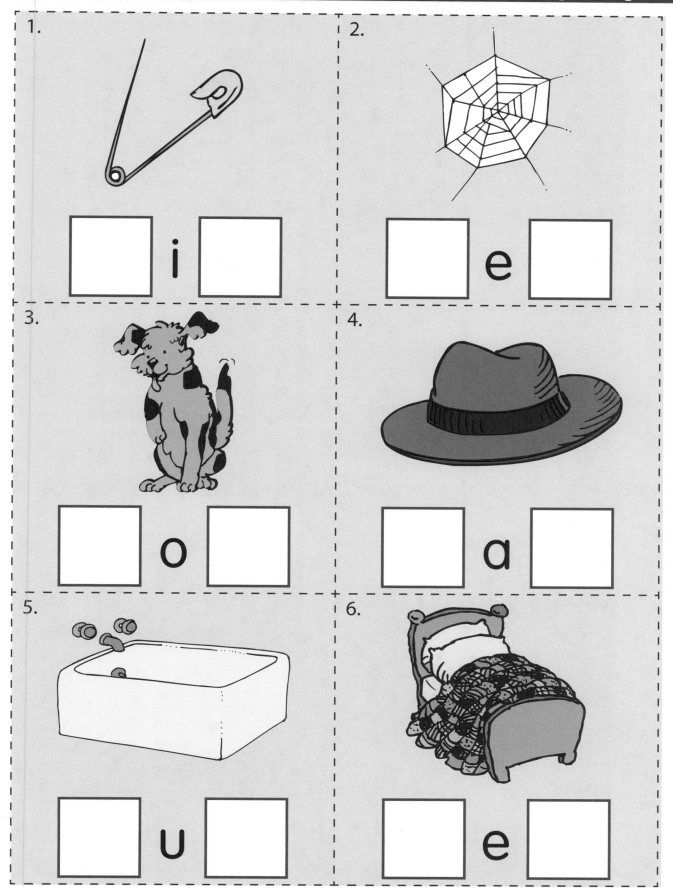

**Identifies Initial and Final
Consonant Sounds**
Phonics

EMC 3338 • © Evan-Moor Corp.

**Identifies Initial and Final
Consonant Sounds**
Phonics

EMC 3338 • © Evan-Moor Corp.

**Identifies Initial and Final
Consonant Sounds**
Phonics

EMC 3338 • © Evan-Moor Corp.

**Identifies Initial and Final
Consonant Sounds**
Phonics

EMC 3338 • © Evan-Moor Corp.

**Identifies Initial and Final
Consonant Sounds**
Phonics

EMC 3338 • © Evan-Moor Corp.

**Identifies Initial and Final
Consonant Sounds**
Phonics

EMC 3338 • © Evan-Moor Corp.

Phonics
Identifies Initial and Final Consonant Sounds

7.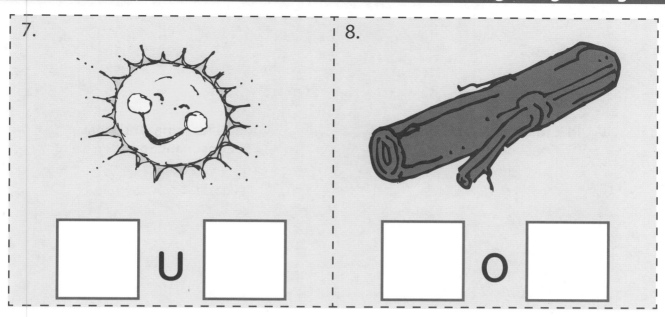

U

8.

O

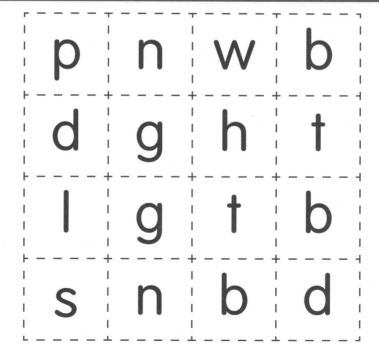

p	n	w	b
d	g	h	t
l	g	t	b
s	n	b	d

Phonics
Identifies Initial and Final Consonant Sounds

**Identifies Initial and Final
Consonant Sounds**

Phonics

EMC 3338 • © Evan-Moor Corp.

**Identifies Initial and Final
Consonant Sounds**

Phonics

EMC 3338 • © Evan-Moor Corp.

**Identifies
Initial & Final
Consonants**
Phonics
EMC 3338
© Evan-Moor Corp.

**Identifies
Initial & Final
Consonants**
Phonics
EMC 3338
© Evan-Moor Corp.

**Identifies
Initial & Final
Consonants**
Phonics
EMC 3338
© Evan-Moor Corp.

**Identifies
Initial & Final
Consonants**
Phonics
EMC 3338
© Evan-Moor Corp.

**Identifies
Initial & Final
Consonants**
Phonics
EMC 3338
© Evan-Moor Corp.

**Identifies
Initial & Final
Consonants**
Phonics
EMC 3338
© Evan-Moor Corp.

**Identifies
Initial & Final
Consonants**
Phonics
EMC 3338
© Evan-Moor Corp.

**Identifies
Initial & Final
Consonants**
Phonics
EMC 3338
© Evan-Moor Corp.

**Identifies
Initial & Final
Consonants**
Phonics
EMC 3338
© Evan-Moor Corp.

**Identifies
Initial & Final
Consonants**
Phonics
EMC 3338
© Evan-Moor Corp.

**Identifies
Initial & Final
Consonants**
Phonics
EMC 3338
© Evan-Moor Corp.

**Identifies
Initial & Final
Consonants**
Phonics
EMC 3338
© Evan-Moor Corp.

**Identifies
Initial & Final
Consonants**
Phonics
EMC 3338
© Evan-Moor Corp.

**Identifies
Initial & Final
Consonants**
Phonics
EMC 3338
© Evan-Moor Corp.

**Identifies
Initial & Final
Consonants**
Phonics
EMC 3338
© Evan-Moor Corp.

**Identifies
Initial & Final
Consonants**
Phonics
EMC 3338
© Evan-Moor Corp.

Identifies Initial and Final Consonant Sounds

Class Checklist		Key:	+ correct response	− incorrect response	• self-corrected				
			i initial consonant	f final consonant					

Name	Date	web	dog	hat	tub	bed	sun	log	Notes
		i/f	i/f	i/f	i/f	i/f	i/f	i/f	
		i/f	i/f	i/f	i/f	i/f	i/f	i/f	
		i/f	i/f	i/f	i/f	i/f	i/f	i/f	
		i/f	i/f	i/f	i/f	i/f	i/f	i/f	
		i/f	i/f	i/f	i/f	i/f	i/f	i/f	
		i/f	i/f	i/f	i/f	i/f	i/f	i/f	
		i/f	i/f	i/f	i/f	i/f	i/f	i/f	
		i/f	i/f	i/f	i/f	i/f	i/f	i/f	
		i/f	i/f	i/f	i/f	i/f	i/f	i/f	
		i/f	i/f	i/f	i/f	i/f	i/f	i/f	
		i/f	i/f	i/f	i/f	i/f	i/f	i/f	
		i/f	i/f	i/f	i/f	i/f	i/f	i/f	
		i/f	i/f	i/f	i/f	i/f	i/f	i/f	
		i/f	i/f	i/f	i/f	i/f	i/f	i/f	
		i/f	i/f	i/f	i/f	i/f	i/f	i/f	
		i/f	i/f	i/f	i/f	i/f	i/f	i/f	
		i/f	i/f	i/f	i/f	i/f	i/f	i/f	
		i/f	i/f	i/f	i/f	i/f	i/f	i/f	
		i/f	i/f	i/f	i/f	i/f	i/f	i/f	
		i/f	i/f	i/f	i/f	i/f	i/f	i/f	
		i/f	i/f	i/f	i/f	i/f	i/f	i/f	
		i/f	i/f	i/f	i/f	i/f	i/f	i/f	

Name _____

Beginning to Ending

Name each picture. Write the letter that stands for the beginning sound.
Write the letter that stands for the ending sound.

1.	2.	3.
☐ i ☐	☐ o ☐	☐ u ☐

4.	5.	6.
☐ a ☐	☐ u ☐	☐ e ☐

7.	8.	9.
☐ a ☐	☐ e ☐	☐ o ☐

Phonics
Identifies Initial and Final Consonant Sounds

Identifies Long Vowel Sounds

Objective:

Student identifies the long vowel sound in a given word.

Materials:

Mat, p. 93

Vowel Cards, p. 93

Class Checklist, p. 95

Activity Sheet, p. 96

Student Task

Place the mat on the table. Lay the vowel cards on the table faceup in a row. Say:

> I will say a word and you will tell me which vowel sound you hear. Let's begin.

Point to picture 1 (cake). Say:

> *Cake.* Which vowel sound do you hear in *cake*?

Student responds. Point to the letter box in picture 1. Say:

> Choose the letter and place it on the mat.

Student responds. Record the student's response on the class checklist. Point to picture 2 (hose). Say:

> *Hose.* Which vowel sound do you hear in *hose*?

Student responds. Point to the letter box in picture 2. Say:

> Choose the letter and place it on the mat.

Student responds. Record the student's response on the class checklist.

Repeat the procedure and the script modeled above for each of the remaining pictures.

Identifies Long Vowel Sounds

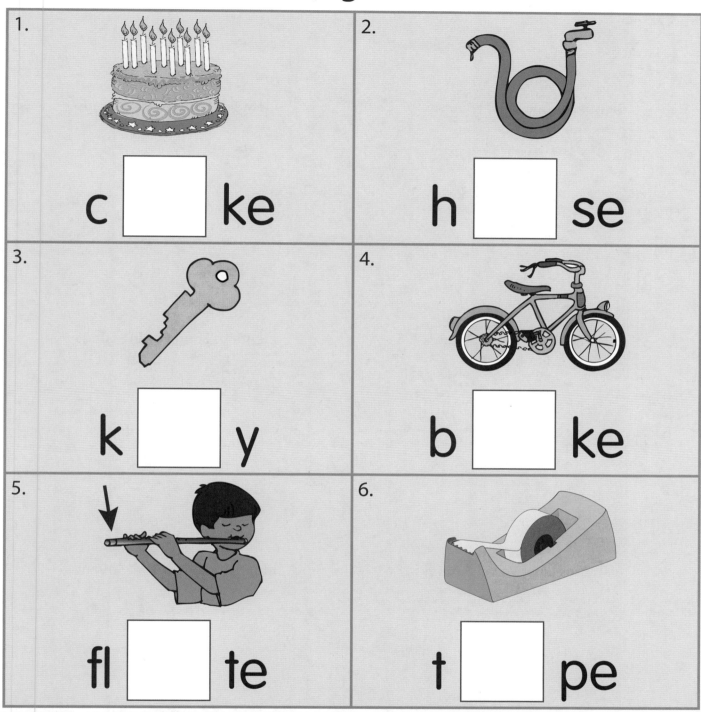

1. c ☐ ke

2. h ☐ se

3. k ☐ y

4. b ☐ ke

5. fl ☐ te

6. t ☐ pe

a   e   i   o   u   a

Identifies Long Vowel Sounds
Phonics

EMC 3338 • © Evan-Moor Corp.

Identifies Long Vowel Sounds
Phonics

EMC 3338 • © Evan-Moor Corp.

Identifies Long Vowel Sounds
Phonics

EMC 3338 • © Evan-Moor Corp.

Identifies Long Vowel Sounds
Phonics

EMC 3338 • © Evan-Moor Corp.

Identifies Long Vowel Sounds
Phonics

EMC 3338 • © Evan-Moor Corp.

Identifies Long Vowel Sounds
Phonics

EMC 3338 • © Evan-Moor Corp.

Identifies Long Vowel Sounds
Phonics
EMC 3338
© Evan-Moor Corp.

Identifies Long Vowel Sounds
Phonics
EMC 3338
© Evan-Moor Corp.

Identifies Long Vowel Sounds
Phonics
EMC 3338
© Evan-Moor Corp.

Identifies Long Vowel Sounds
Phonics
EMC 3338
© Evan-Moor Corp.

Identifies Long Vowel Sounds
Phonics
EMC 3338
© Evan-Moor Corp.

Identifies Long Vowel Sounds
Phonics
EMC 3338
© Evan-Moor Corp.

Identifies Long Vowel Sounds

Class Checklist		Key: + correct response − incorrect response • self-corrected						
Name	Date	cake a	hose o	key e	bike i	flute u	tape a	Notes

Phonics
Identifies Long Vowel Sounds

Activity Shee

Name _____

Which Long Vowel?
a, e, i, o, u

Name each picture.
Write the letter or letters that stand for the vowel sound you hear.

1.	2.	3.
r___se	b___ke	d___ce
4.	**5.**	**6.**
t___pe	j___ ___p	pl___te
7.	**8.**	**9.**
n___ne	h___se	fl___te

Phonics

Identifies the Sounds Made by Long Vowel Digraphs

Objective:
Student listens to a word and identifies the sound made by the long vowel digraph.

Materials:
Mat, p. 99
Word Cards, p. 101
Class Checklist, p. 103
Activity Sheet, p. 104

Student Task

Place the mat on the table. Put the word cards in numerical order in a pile on the table. Say:

> Some words have two vowels that make one sound.

> I will say a word, and you will tell me which long vowel sound you hear. Let's begin.

Place card 1 (bee) on the table. Say:

> *Bee.* Do you hear long *a*, long *o*, or long *e* in *bee*?

Student responds. Say:

> Place the card on the mat under the vowel sound you hear.

Record the student's response on the class checklist. Place card 2 (leaf) on the table. Say:

> *Leaf.* Which long vowel sound do you hear in *leaf*?

Student responds.

> Place the card on the mat under the vowel sound you hear.

Record the student's response on the class checklist. Place card 3 (nail) on the table. Say:

> *Nail.* Which long vowel sound do you hear in *nail*?

Student responds.

> Place the card on the mat under the vowel sound you hear.

Record the student's response on the class checklist.

Repeat the procedure and the script modeled above for each of the remaining cards.

Phonics

Long Vowel Digraphs

ē	ā	ō

**Identifies the Sounds Made by
Long Vowel Digraphs**

Phonics

EMC 3338 • © Evan-Moor Corp.

1. b**ee**

2. l**ea**f

3. n**ai**l

4. f**ee**t

5. b**ea**n

6. tr**ay**

7. r**ai**n

8. h**ay**

9. t**oe**

10. g**oa**t

11. b**ow**

12. c**oa**t

**Identifies the Sounds Made
by Long Vowel Digraphs**
Phonics

EMC 3338 • © Evan-Moor Corp.

**Identifies the Sounds Made
by Long Vowel Digraphs**
Phonics

EMC 3338 • © Evan-Moor Corp.

**Identifies the Sounds Made
by Long Vowel Digraphs**
Phonics

EMC 3338 • © Evan-Moor Corp.

**Identifies the Sounds Made
by Long Vowel Digraphs**
Phonics

EMC 3338 • © Evan-Moor Corp.

**Identifies the Sounds Made
by Long Vowel Digraphs**
Phonics

EMC 3338 • © Evan-Moor Corp.

**Identifies the Sounds Made
by Long Vowel Digraphs**
Phonics

EMC 3338 • © Evan-Moor Corp.

**Identifies the Sounds Made
by Long Vowel Digraphs**
Phonics

EMC 3338 • © Evan-Moor Corp.

**Identifies the Sounds Made
by Long Vowel Digraphs**
Phonics

EMC 3338 • © Evan-Moor Corp.

**Identifies the Sounds Made
by Long Vowel Digraphs**
Phonics

EMC 3338 • © Evan-Moor Corp.

**Identifies the Sounds Made
by Long Vowel Digraphs**
Phonics

EMC 3338 • © Evan-Moor Corp.

**Identifies the Sounds Made
by Long Vowel Digraphs**
Phonics

EMC 3338 • © Evan-Moor Corp.

**Identifies the Sounds Made
by Long Vowel Digraphs**
Phonics

EMC 3338 • © Evan-Moor Corp.

Identifies the Sounds Made by Long Vowel Digraphs

Class Checklist		Key: + correct response − incorrect response ● self-corrected						
Name	Date	bee, feet $\bar{e}$	leaf, bean $\bar{e}$	nail, rain $\bar{a}$	hay, tray $\bar{a}$	goat, coat $\bar{o}$	bow $\bar{o}$	toe $\bar{o}$

Name _____

Two Letters Make One Sound

Name each picture.
Circle the letters in each word that make the long vowel sound.

oa   ow   oe   ee   ea   ai   ay   ie

1. coat	2. jeep	3. bow
4. rain	5. goat	6. hay
7. leaf	8. toe	9. tie

Discriminates "R-Controlled" Words

Objective:
Student categorizes -*er*, -*ir*, -*ar*, and -*or* words.

Materials:
Mat, p. 107
Picture Cards, p. 109
Class Checklist, p. 111
Activity Sheet, p. 112

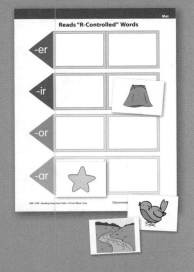

Model the Task

Place the mat on the table. Place the picture cards faceup in a pile. Place the star card at the top of the pile and the bird card next so you can readily choose them. Say:

> We are going to listen for different /r/ sounds in words.

Choose the star picture card and place it on the table. Say:

> *star*

Point to each box on the mat as you talk about it. Say:

> Do we hear the -*er* sound, the -*ir* sound, the -*or* sound, or the -*ar* sound in the word *star*?

Student may respond or you may answer. Say:

> *Star.* I hear the -*ar* sound in the word *star*. So I put the card next to -*ar* on the mat.

Student Task

Place the bird card on the table. Say:

> *Bird.* Which /r/ sound do you hear in *bird*?

Student responds. Say:

> Place the card on the mat next to the /r/ sound you hear.

Student responds.

Repeat the procedure and the script modeled above for each of the remaining picture cards. Use the mat as a reference to record the student's responses on the class checklist.

Reads "R-Controlled" Words

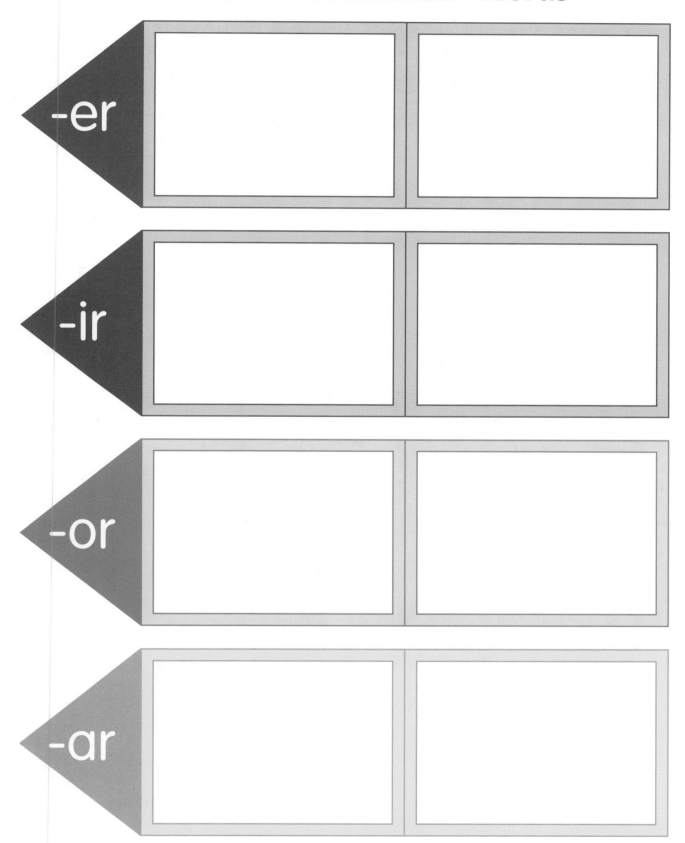

-er

-ir

-or

-ar

Phonics
Discriminates "R-Controlled" Words   **107**

Discriminates "R-Controlled" Words
Phonics

EMC 3338 • © Evan-Moor Corp.

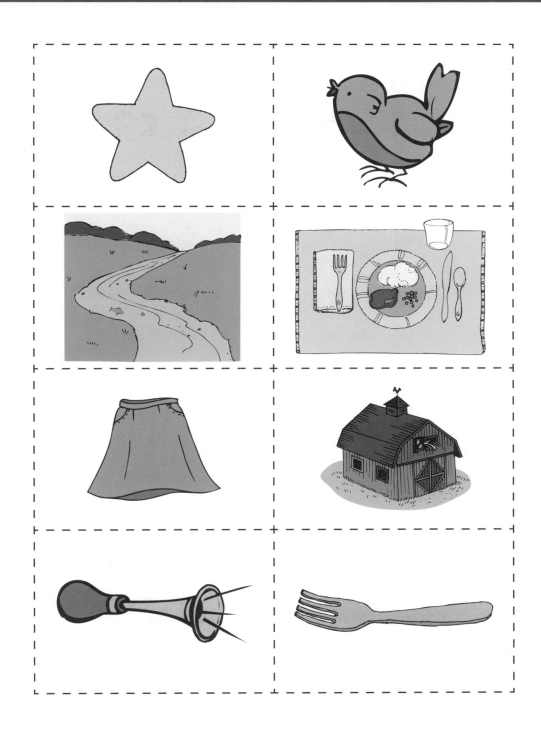

Phonics
Discriminates "R-Controlled" Words **109**

bird

**Discriminates
"R-Controlled" Words**

Phonics

EMC 3338 • © Evan-Moor Corp.

star

**Discriminates
"R-Controlled" Words**

Phonics

EMC 3338 • © Evan-Moor Corp.

dinner

**Discriminates
"R-Controlled" Words**

Phonics

EMC 3338 • © Evan-Moor Corp.

river

**Discriminates
"R-Controlled" Words**

Phonics

EMC 3338 • © Evan-Moor Corp.

barn

**Discriminates
"R-Controlled" Words**

Phonics

EMC 3338 • © Evan-Moor Corp.

skirt

**Discriminates
"R-Controlled" Words**

Phonics

EMC 3338 • © Evan-Moor Corp.

fork

**Discriminates
"R-Controlled" Words**

Phonics

EMC 3338 • © Evan-Moor Corp.

horn

**Discriminates
"R-Controlled" Words**

Phonics

EMC 3338 • © Evan-Moor Corp.

Discriminates "R-Controlled" Words

Class Checklist			Key:	+ correct response	− incorrect response			• self-corrected			
Name	Date	star -ar	bird -ir	river -er	dinner -er	skirt -ir	barn -ar	horn -or	fork -or		Notes

Note: Student names each picture and fills in a circle to indicate the correct /r/ sound.
1. star, 2. girl, 3. bird, 4. horn, 5. dinner, 6. yarn, 7. shirt, 8. turtle, 9. jar

Which Do You Hear?

Name each picture.
Fill in the circle below the sound you hear.

1.	2.	3.
-ar -ir -ur	-ar -or -ir	-ar -ir -ur
○ ○ ○	○ ○ ○	○ ○ ○

4.	5.	6.
-ar -or -ir	-er -or -ur	-ar -or -ur
○ ○ ○	○ ○ ○	○ ○ ○

7.	8.	9.
-ar -or -ir	-er -or -ur	-ar -ir -ur
○ ○ ○	○ ○ ○	○ ○ ○

Reads and Identifies Contractions

Objective:
Student reads contractions and identifies words that make up the contraction.

Materials:
Mat, p. 115

Word Cards, p. 117

Class Checklist, p. 119

Activity Sheet, p. 120

Model the Task

Place the mat on the table. Place the word cards in a pile on the table. Say:

> I am going to read a contraction. Then I will find the words that make the contraction.

Place the *wasn't* word card on the table. Say:

> *Wasn't.* The words *was* and *not* make up the word *wasn't.*

Place the card under *was not* on the mat. Say:

> So I put the card under the words *was not.*

Student Task

> Now it's your turn. Choose a card, read it to me, and find the words that make the contraction. Let's begin.

Student chooses a card and reads the contraction aloud. Say:

> Now place the card on the mat under the two words that make the contraction.

Student responds. Repeat the procedure and the script modeled above for each of the remaining word cards. Use the mat as a reference to record the student's responses on the class checklist.

Contractions

| was not | it is | I will |

| she is | can not | he is |

| we will | you will | do not |

Phonics
Reads and Identifies Contractions   **115**

Reads and Identifies Contractions
Phonics

EMC 3338 • © Evan-Moor Corp.

wasn't	it's	I'll
she's	can't	he's
we'll	you'll	don't

**Reads and
Identifies
Contractions**

Phonics

EMC 3338 • © Evan-Moor Corp.

**Reads and
Identifies
Contractions**

Phonics

EMC 3338 • © Evan-Moor Corp.

**Reads and
Identifies
Contractions**

Phonics

EMC 3338 • © Evan-Moor Corp.

**Reads and
Identifies
Contractions**

Phonics

EMC 3338 • © Evan-Moor Corp.

**Reads and
Identifies
Contractions**

Phonics

EMC 3338 • © Evan-Moor Corp.

**Reads and
Identifies
Contractions**

Phonics

EMC 3338 • © Evan-Moor Corp.

**Reads and
Identifies
Contractions**

Phonics

EMC 3338 • © Evan-Moor Corp.

**Reads and
Identifies
Contractions**

Phonics

EMC 3338 • © Evan-Moor Corp.

**Reads and
Identifies
Contractions**

Phonics

EMC 3338 • © Evan-Moor Corp.

Reads and Identifies Contractions

Class Checklist											Key: + correct response — incorrect response ● self-corrected	
Name	Date	wasn't	it's	I'll	she's	can't	he's	we'll	you'll	don't	Notes	

Name _____

Correct Contractions

Circle the contraction.
Underline the two words that make the contraction.

1.

   He's a fun boy.   He is

                                       It is

2.

   I don't like bugs.   will not

                                     do not

3.

   She can't come.   can not

                                     I will

4.

   You'll go home.   You will

                                     She is

5.

   It's not mine.   It is

                                     You are

Reads Compound Words

Objective:
Student makes and reads compound words.

Materials:
Word Cards, p. 123

Class Checklist, p. 125

Activity Sheet, p. 126

Student Task

Place the word cards in random order faceup on the table. Say:

> A compound word is two words put together to make one new word.

> Look at the word cards. You are going to put together two word cards to make a compound word. Let's begin.

> Choose two word cards that make a compound word.

Student chooses two word cards to make a familiar compound word. Say:

> Read the word to me.

Student responds. Record the student's response on the class checklist. Say:

> Now make another compound word and read the word to me.

Student responds. Record the student's response on the class checklist.

Repeat the procedure and the script modeled above until the student has matched all the word cards to make compound words.

pop corn

pan cake

snow man

gold fish

Reads Compound Words
Phonics

EMC 3338 • © Evan-Moor Corp.

Reads Compound Words
Phonics

EMC 3338 • © Evan-Moor Corp.

Reads Compound Words
Phonics

EMC 3338 • © Evan-Moor Corp.

Reads Compound Words
Phonics

EMC 3338 • © Evan-Moor Corp.

Reads Compound Words
Phonics

EMC 3338 • © Evan-Moor Corp.

Reads Compound Words
Phonics

EMC 3338 • © Evan-Moor Corp.

Reads Compound Words
Phonics

EMC 3338 • © Evan-Moor Corp.

Reads Compound Words
Phonics

EMC 3338 • © Evan-Moor Corp.

Reads Compound Words

Class Checklist		Key: + correct response − incorrect response ● self-corrected				
Name	Date	popcorn	pancake	snowman	goldfish	Notes

Note: Student makes compound words.

Name _____

Finish It

Write a word from the box to complete each compound word.

house	bow	shell
ball	day	plane

rain _____

air _____

birth _____

sea _____

dog _____

foot _____

Phonics

Reads Inflectional Forms and Root Words

Objective:
Student reads words with
-*s*, -*ed*, and -*ing* endings.

Materials:
Mat, p. 129
Word Cards, p. 131
Class Checklist, p. 133
Activity Sheet, p. 134

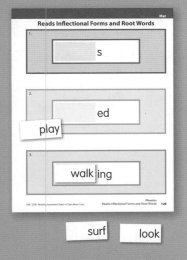

Model the Task

Place the mat on the table. Place the word cards faceup in a pile on the table. Place the *melt* word card at the top of the pile. Say:

> One word can have different endings. Look at the word *melt*. I will place it on the mat next to an ending and read the word to you.

Place the *melt* word card next to *s* on the mat. Say:

> *melts*

Place the *melt* card next to *ed* on the mat. Say:

> *melted*

Place the *melt* card next to *ing* on the mat. Say:

> *melting*

Student Task

> Now it's your turn. Let's begin. Choose a card and read the word to me.

Student responds. Say:

> Now place it next to *s* on the mat and read the word to me.

Student responds. Say:

> Place it next to *ed* and read the word to me.

Student responds. Say:

> Now place it next to *ing* and read the word to me.

Student responds. Record the student's responses on the class checklist.

Repeat the procedure and the script modeled above for each of the remaining word cards.

Reads Inflectional Forms and Root Words

1.

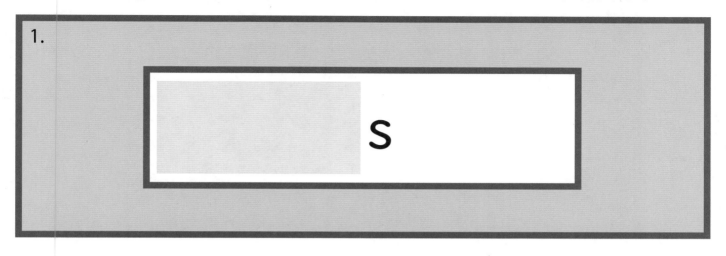

s

2.

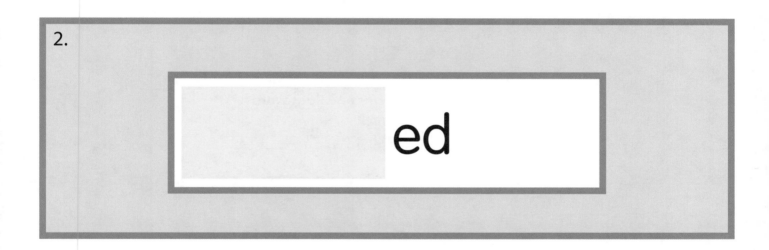

ed

3.

ing

Reads Inflectional Forms and Root Words
Phonics

EMC 3338 • © Evan-Moor Corp.

play	walk	jump
look	melt	kick
surf	burn	pack

Phonics
Reads Inflectional Forms and Root Words **131**

**Reads Inflectional Forms
and Root Words**
Phonics

EMC 3338 • © Evan-Moor Corp.

**Reads Inflectional Forms
and Root Words**
Phonics

EMC 3338 • © Evan-Moor Corp.

**Reads Inflectional Forms
and Root Words**
Phonics

EMC 3338 • © Evan-Moor Corp.

**Reads Inflectional Forms
and Root Words**
Phonics

EMC 3338 • © Evan-Moor Corp.

**Reads Inflectional Forms
and Root Words**
Phonics

EMC 3338 • © Evan-Moor Corp.

**Reads Inflectional Forms
and Root Words**
Phonics

EMC 3338 • © Evan-Moor Corp.

**Reads Inflectional Forms
and Root Words**
Phonics

EMC 3338 • © Evan-Moor Corp.

**Reads Inflectional Forms
and Root Words**
Phonics

EMC 3338 • © Evan-Moor Corp.

**Reads Inflectional Forms
and Root Words**
Phonics

EMC 3338 • © Evan-Moor Corp.

Reads Inflectional Forms and Root Words

Class Checklist		Key:	+ correct response		– incorrect response		● self-corrected			
Name	Date	walk	jump	look	kick	surf	play	burn	pack	Notes

Note: Student chooses the correct word to complete each sentence.

Name _____

Fill It In

Write the word that correctly completes the sentence.

1. I am _____ outside.

sit

sitting

2. She _____ ball.

play

played

3. Mom _____ hugs.

like

likes

4. It _____ yesterday.

rained

rains

5. He is _____ up and down.

jumping

jumps

6. The bird _____ to me.

singing

sings

Reads Common Word Families

Objective:
Student reads words in common word families.

Materials:
Mat, p. 137
Word Cards, p. 139
Class Checklist, p. 141
Activity Sheet, p. 142

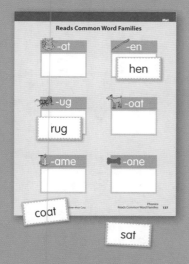

Model the Task

Place the mat and the word cards faceup in a pile on the table. Place the *sat* word card at the top of the pile. Say:

> We are going to sort words into word families. Look at the mat. It shows six word family endings.

Point to each word family ending as you read it to the student. Say:

> *-at, -en, -ug, -oat, -ame, -one*

> I am going to pick one word card from the pile. I will read the word and place the card in the correct word family.

Pick the *sat* word card from the pile, read it aloud, and place it under the *-at* family on the mat. Say:

> *Sat.* The word *sat* is in the *-at* word family, so I put it under *-at* on the mat.

Student Task

> Now it's your turn. Let's begin.
> Choose a card and read the word to me.

Student responds.

> Now place the word under its word family on the mat.

Student responds. Record the student's response on the class checklist.

> Choose another card, read the word to me, and place it under its word family.

Record the student's response on the class checklist.

Student continues at his or her own pace until all the cards are sorted on the mat.

Reads Common Word Families

 -at

 -en

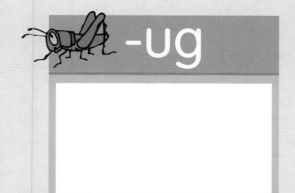 -ug

 -oat

 -ame

 -one

Reads Common Word Families
Phonics

EMC 3338 • © Evan-Moor Corp.

sat	hat	bat
hen	ten	den
rug	mug	hug
coat	boat	float
name	fame	game
cone	tone	stone

**Reads Common
Word Families**

Phonics

EMC 3338 • © Evan-Moor Corp.

**Reads Common
Word Families**

Phonics

EMC 3338 • © Evan-Moor Corp.

**Reads Common
Word Families**

Phonics

EMC 3338 • © Evan-Moor Corp.

**Reads Common
Word Families**

Phonics

EMC 3338 • © Evan-Moor Corp.

**Reads Common
Word Families**

Phonics

EMC 3338 • © Evan-Moor Corp.

**Reads Common
Word Families**

Phonics

EMC 3338 • © Evan-Moor Corp.

**Reads Common
Word Families**

Phonics

EMC 3338 • © Evan-Moor Corp.

**Reads Common
Word Families**

Phonics

EMC 3338 • © Evan-Moor Corp.

**Reads Common
Word Families**

Phonics

EMC 3338 • © Evan-Moor Corp.

**Reads Common
Word Families**

Phonics

EMC 3338 • © Evan-Moor Corp.

**Reads Common
Word Families**

Phonics

EMC 3338 • © Evan-Moor Corp.

**Reads Common
Word Families**

Phonics

EMC 3338 • © Evan-Moor Corp.

**Reads Common
Word Families**

Phonics

EMC 3338 • © Evan-Moor Corp.

**Reads Common
Word Families**

Phonics

EMC 3338 • © Evan-Moor Corp.

**Reads Common
Word Families**

Phonics

EMC 3338 • © Evan-Moor Corp.

**Reads Common
Word Families**

Phonics

EMC 3338 • © Evan-Moor Corp.

**Reads Common
Word Families**

Phonics

EMC 3338 • © Evan-Moor Corp.

**Reads Common
Word Families**

Phonics

EMC 3338 • © Evan-Moor Corp.

Reads Common Word Families

Class Checklist		Key: + correct response − incorrect response ● self-corrected						

Name	Date	**-at** sat, hat, bat	**-en** hen, ten, den	**-ug** rug, mug, hug	**-oat** coat, boat, float	**-ame** name, fame, game	**-one** cone, tone, stone	Notes

Note: Student writes each word in the correct word family group.

Name _____

In the Family

Write each word under the picture in the same word family.

bake	cone	lake	tap
bug	clap	plate	hug
cat	gate	sat	stone

1. rug

_____

_____

2. map

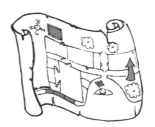

_____

_____

3. skate

_____

_____

4. bat

_____

_____

5. bone

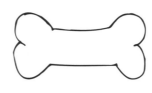

_____

_____

6. cake

_____

_____

Quick Checks

Unit 4

Vocabulary & Concept Development/Reading Comprehension

Classifies Categories of Words

Objective:
Student reads words and sorts them into categories.

Materials:
Category Cards, p. 147

Word Cards, p. 147

Class Checklist, p. 149

Activity Sheet, p. 150

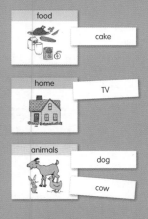

Model the Task

Place the category cards in a row in the order of *food, home,* and *animals.* Leave space between each category card. The student will place each word card below the correct category card. Spread the word cards faceup on the table. Say:

> Today we are going to read words and sort them into groups.

Point to each category card as you name it. Say:

> The groups are *food, home,* and *animals.*

> Look at the word cards. Some of the words belong in the *food* group, some belong in the *home* group, and some belong in the *animals* group.

Choose the *toys* word card and place it below the *home* category card. Say:

> *Toys.* This card belongs in the *home* group because you find toys in a home.

Student Task

> Now you read each word and place it in one of the groups.

Allow the student to sort the word cards at his or her own pace. You may assist the student in reading a word. Record the student's placements on the class checklist once all the cards have been categorized.

Classifies Categories of Words

food

home

animals

cow

TV

dog

cake

hot dog

toys

apple

bed

pig

Classifies Categories of Words

Vocabulary & Concept
Development/Reading Comprehension

EMC 3338 • © Evan-Moor Corp.

Classifies Categories of Words

Vocabulary & Concept
Development/Reading Comprehension

EMC 3338 • © Evan-Moor Corp.

Classifies Categories of Words

Vocabulary & Concept
Development/Reading Comprehension

EMC 3338 • © Evan-Moor Corp.

Classifies Categories of Words

Vocabulary & Concept
Development/Reading Comprehension

EMC 3338 • © Evan-Moor Corp.

Classifies Categories of Words

Vocabulary & Concept
Development/Reading Comprehension

EMC 3338 • © Evan-Moor Corp.

Classifies Categories of Words

Vocabulary & Concept
Development/Reading Comprehension

EMC 3338 • © Evan-Moor Corp.

Classifies Categories of Words

Vocabulary & Concept
Development/Reading Comprehension

EMC 3338 • © Evan-Moor Corp.

Classifies Categories of Words

Vocabulary & Concept
Development/Reading Comprehension

EMC 3338 • © Evan-Moor Corp.

Classifies Categories of Words

Vocabulary & Concept
Development/Reading Comprehension

EMC 3338 • © Evan-Moor Corp.

Classifies Categories of Words

Vocabulary & Concept
Development/Reading Comprehension

EMC 3338 • © Evan-Moor Corp.

Classifies Categories of Words

Vocabulary & Concept
Development/Reading Comprehension

EMC 3338 • © Evan-Moor Corp.

Classifies Categories of Words

Vocabulary & Concept
Development/Reading Comprehension

EMC 3338 • © Evan-Moor Corp.

Classifies Categories of Words

Class Checklist		Key: + correct response − incorrect response • self-corrected			
Name	Date	food	home	animals	Notes

Vocabulary & Concept Development/Reading Comprehension

Name _____

Where Does Each Belong?

Cut out and glue each word card into the correct group.

Vocabulary & Concept Development/Reading Comprehension

Objective:
Student reads a list of 24 of the most frequently used words.

Materials:
Mat, p. 153
Class Checklist, p. 155
Activity Sheet, p. 156

Student Task

Place the mat on the table in front of the student. You may wish to use a bookmark to isolate each word the student is reading. Say:

Read each word on the mat to me. Let's begin.

Isolate each word on the mat. Record any words the student does not read correctly on the class checklist.

High-Frequency Words

the	of	and
to	in	you
for	it	was
on	that	is
he	are	as
his	they	with
this	from	at
by	one	had

High-Frequency Words

the	of	and
to	in	you
for	it	was
on	that	is
he	are	as
his	they	with
this	from	at
by	one	had

153

Reads High-Frequency Words

Vocabulary & Concept Development/Reading Comprehension

EMC 3338 • © Evan-Moor Corp.

Reads High-Frequency Words

Class Checklist		Record any words the student misread.	
Name	Date	Words Student Cannot Read	Notes

Name _____

Finish It

Circle the word that correctly completes each sentence.

1.

_____ cat sat.

In   The

2.

This is for _____.

you   on

3.

He _____ a pig.

are   had

4.

My dog has _____ spot.

one   by

5.

I will go _____ bed.

to   of

6.

She is _____ me.

was   with

Sequences/Logical Order

Objective:
Student reads sentence cards and puts them in sequential order.

Materials:
Mats, pp. 159 and 161

Sentence Cards, pp. 159 and 161

Class Checklist, p. 163

Activity Sheet, p. 164

Student Task

Place one story mat on the table. Place the accompanying sentence cards faceup in random order next to the mat. Say:

> Look at the picture on the mat. Then read each sentence card and place the cards on the mat to show what happens first, next, then, and last.

Student places the sentence cards in sequential order. Record the student's response on the class checklist. Say:

> Now read the story to me.

Student reads the story aloud.

You may wish to use the additional story for retesting purposes.

The Note

1 glue
2 glue
3 glue
4 glue

Pam asked her mom. Her mom said yes.	Pam got a note.
It was from Jill.	The note said, "Can you sleep at my house?"

Vocabulary & Concept Development/Reading Comprehension
Sequences/Logical Order

Sequences/Logical Order

Vocabulary & Concept Development/Reading Comprehension

EMC 3338 • © Evan-Moor Corp.

Sequences/Logical Order

Vocabulary & Concept
Development/Reading Comprehension

EMC 3338 • © Evan-Moor Corp.

Sequences/Logical Order

Vocabulary & Concept
Development/Reading Comprehension

EMC 3338 • © Evan-Moor Corp.

Sequences/Logical Order

Vocabulary & Concept
Development/Reading Comprehension

EMC 3338 • © Evan-Moor Corp.

Sequences/Logical Order

Vocabulary & Concept
Development/Reading Comprehension

EMC 3338 • © Evan-Moor Corp.

The First Day of School

1 glue	
2 glue	
3 glue	
4 glue	
5 glue	
6 glue	

Get dressed.	Find the classroom.
Meet the teacher.	Wake up.
Ride the bus.	Then eat breakfast.

Vocabulary & Concept Development/Reading Comprehension
Sequences/Logical Order **161**

Sequences/Logical Order
Vocabulary & Concept Development/Reading Comprehension

EMC 3338 • © Evan-Moor Corp.

Sequences/Logical Order
Vocabulary & Concept
Development/Reading Comprehension
EMC 3338 • © Evan-Moor Corp.

Sequences/Logical Order
Vocabulary & Concept
Development/Reading Comprehension
EMC 3338 • © Evan-Moor Corp.

Sequences/Logical Order
Vocabulary & Concept
Development/Reading Comprehension
EMC 3338 • © Evan-Moor Corp.

Sequences/Logical Order
Vocabulary & Concept
Development/Reading Comprehension
EMC 3338 • © Evan-Moor Corp.

Sequences/Logical Order
Vocabulary & Concept
Development/Reading Comprehension
EMC 3338 • © Evan-Moor Corp.

Sequences/Logical Order
Vocabulary & Concept
Development/Reading Comprehension
EMC 3338 • © Evan-Moor Corp.

Sequences/Logical Order

Class Checklist		Key: + correct response − incorrect response ● self-corrected	
Name	Date	Story: The Note	Story: The First Day of School

Vocabulary & Concept Development/Reading Comprehension

Note: Student cuts and glues the pictures in order. Then the student writes sentences for the pictures.

Name _____

Be a Clown

Cut out the pictures. Glue them in order.
Write sentences that tell about each picture.

1 glue	_____ _____ _____
2 glue	_____ _____ _____
3 glue	_____ _____ _____

Vocabulary & Concept Development/Reading Comprehension
EMC 3338 • Reading Assessment Tasks • © Evan-Moor Corp.

Responds to Who, What, Where, When, and How Questions

Objective:

Student answers who, what, where, when, and how questions about a story.

Materials:

Class Checklist, p. 167

Activity Sheet, p. 168

Auditory Only

Student Task

Say:

> Listen carefully while I read you a story. Then I will ask you questions about the story. Let's begin.
>
> There once was a pig named Muffin. Every morning, Muffin walked to a bakery in the city. The bakery workers gave him muffins to munch. He ate big muffins, small muffins, half muffins, and whole muffins. I bet you know how Muffin got his name!

A reasonable answer is recorded as *correct* and an unreasonable answer is recorded as *incorrect*. Say:

> Who was the story about?

Student responds. Record the student's response on the class checklist. Say:

> What did Muffin do?

Student responds. Record the student's response on the class checklist. Say:

> Where is the bakery?

Student responds. Record the student's response on the class checklist. Say:

> When did Muffin walk to the bakery?

Student responds. Record the student's response on the class checklist. Say:

> How do you think Muffin got his name?

Student responds. Record the student's response on the class checklist.

Responds to Factual Questions

Class Checklist							Key: **+** correct response **−** incorrect response **●** self-corrected
Name	Date	Who	What	Where	When	How	Notes

Vocabulary & Concept Development/Reading Comprehension

Note: Student answers factual questions.

Name _____

Read. Write.

Sam

Sam is a dog.
Sam can wag.
Sam can run fast.
Sam can dig.

Who?  _____ is a dog.

What?  Sam can _____.

How?  Sam can run _____.

Draw a picture to show where Sam is.

Makes Predictions About What Will Happen Next

Objective:
Student predicts what will happen next in a story.

Materials:
Class Checklist, p. 171

Activity Sheet, p. 172

Auditory Only

Student Task

Say:

> Listen carefully while I read you a story. Then tell me what you think will happen next in the story. Let's begin.

> Lucy was always late for school. Her old alarm clock never went off on time. Lucy decided that she could not be late for school anymore. She went to the store and bought a new alarm clock.

> What do you think happened next?

Student responds. Record the student's response on the class checklist.

Makes Predictions About What Will Happen Next

Class Checklist		Key: + correct response − incorrect response • self-corrected
Name	Date	Note Responses

Vocabulary & Concept Development/Reading Comprehension

Name _____

What Will Happen Next?

Read the story.
Draw a picture to tell what will happen next.

Mama Bird sits.

The egg sits.

The egg cracks.

Draw what will happen next.

Vocabulary & Concept Development/Reading Comprehension

Answer Key

Page 14

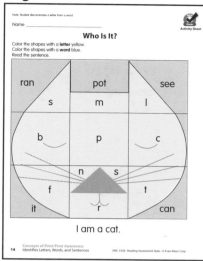

Page 34

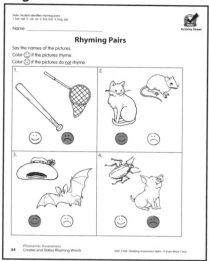

Page 38

Page 42

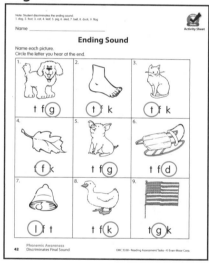

Page 46

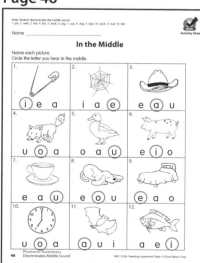

Page 54

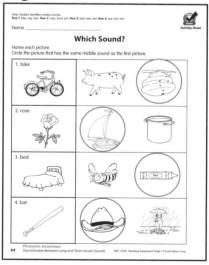

Page 58

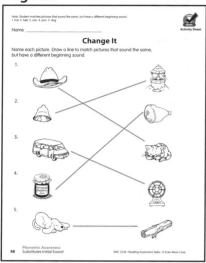

Page 62

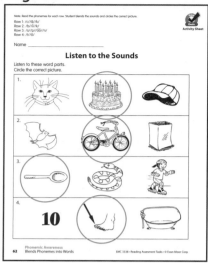

Page 68

Page 74

Page 82

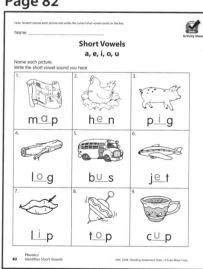

Page 90

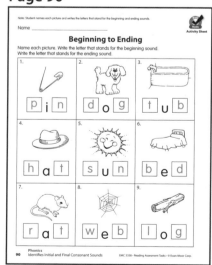

Page 96

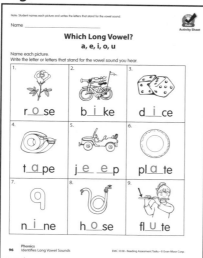

Name _____

Which Long Vowel?
a, e, i, o, u

Name each picture.
Write the letter or letters that stand for the vowel sound you hear.

1. r o se	2. b i ke	3. d i ce
4. t a pe	5. j ee p	6. pl a te
7. n i ne	8. h o se	9. fl u te

96 Phonics
Identifies Long Vowel Sounds   EMC 3338 • Reading Assessment Tasks • © Evan-Moor Corp.

Page 104

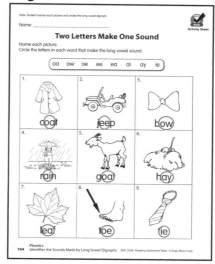

Name _____

Two Letters Make One Sound

Name each picture.
Circle the letters in each word that make the long vowel sound.

oa   ow   oe   ee   ea   ai   ay   ie

1. coat	2. jeep	3. bow
4. rain	5. goat	6. hay
7. leaf	8. toe	9. tie

104 Phonics
Identifies the Sounds Made by Long Vowel Digraphs   EMC 3338 • Reading Assessment Tasks • © Evan-Moor Corp.

Page 112

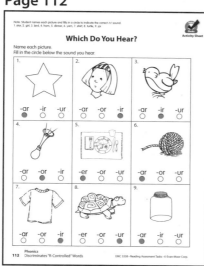

Name _____

Which Do You Hear?

Name each picture.
Fill in the circle below the sound you hear.

1. -ar ○ -ir ○ -ur ○	2. -ar ○ -or ○ -ir ○	3. -ar ○ -ir ○ -ur ○
4. -ar ○ -or ○ -ir ○	5. -er ○ -or ○ -ur ○	6. -ar ○ -or ○ -ur ○
7. -ar ○ -or ○ -ir ○	8. -er ○ -or ○ -ur ○	9. -ar ○ -ir ○ -ur ○

112 Phonics
Discriminates "R-Controlled" Words   EMC 3338 • Reading Assessment Tasks • © Evan-Moor Corp.

Page 120

Name _____

Correct Contractions

Circle the contraction.
Underline the two words that make the contraction.

1. He's a fun boy.   He is
                            It is

2. I don't like bugs.   will not
                            do not

3. She can't come.   can not
                            I will

4. You'll go home.   You will
                            She is

5. It's not mine.   It is
                            You are

120 Phonics
Reads and Identifies Contractions   EMC 3338 • Reading Assessment Tasks • © Evan-Moor Corp.

Page 126

Name _____

Finish It

Write a word from the box to complete each compound word.

house   bow   shell
ball   day   plane

rain bow
air plane
birth day
sea shell
dog house
foot ball

126 Phonics
Reads Compound Words   EMC 3338 • Reading Assessment Tasks • © Evan-Moor Corp.

Page 134

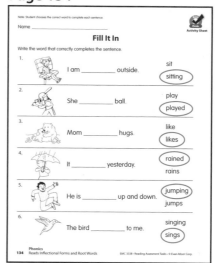

Name _____

Fill It In

Write the word that correctly completes the sentence.

1. I am _____ outside.   sit (sitting)
2. She _____ ball.   play (played)
3. Mom _____ hugs.   like (likes)
4. It _____ yesterday.   (rained) rains
5. He is _____ up and down. (jumping) jumps
6. The bird _____ to me.   singing (sings)

134 Phonics
Reads Inflectional Forms and Root Words   EMC 3338 • Reading Assessment Tasks • © Evan-Moor Corp.

Page 142

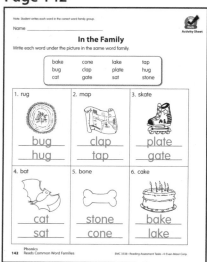

In the Family

Write each word under the picture in the same word family.

bake	cone	lake	tap
bug	clap	plate	hug
cat	gate	sat	stone

1. rug — bug, hug
2. map — clap, tap
3. skate — plate, gate
4. bat — cat, sat
5. bone — stone, cone
6. cake — bake, lake

Page 150

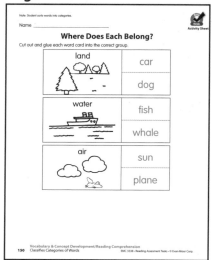

Where Does Each Belong?

Cut out and glue each word card into the correct group.

land — car, dog
water — fish, whale
air — sun, plane

Page 156

Finish It

Circle the word that correctly completes each sentence.

1. ___ cat sat. In / (The)
2. This is for ___. (you) / on
3. He ___ a pig. are / (had)
4. My dog has ___ spot. (one) / by
5. I will go ___ bed. (to) / of
6. She is ___ me. was / (with)

Page 164

Be a Clown

Cut out the pictures. Glue them in order.
Write sentences that tell about each picture.

Sentences will vary.

Page 168

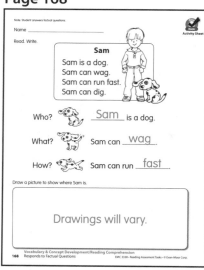

Sam

Sam is a dog.
Sam can wag.
Sam can run fast.
Sam can dig.

Who? Sam is a dog.
What? Sam can wag.
How? Sam can run fast.

Draw a picture to show where Sam is.

Drawings will vary.

Page 172

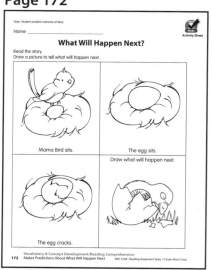

What Will Happen Next?

Read the story.
Draw a picture to tell what will happen next.

Mama Bird sits.
The egg sits.
The egg cracks.
Draw what will happen next.